SPECIAL

THE OPEN MEDIA PAMPHLET SERIES

EDITION

OTHER OPEN MEDIA PAMPHLET SERIES TITLES

CORPORATE MEDIA AND THE THREAT TO DEMOCRACY
Robert W. McChesney
80 pages / $5.95 / ISBN: 1-888363-47-9

THE WTO: FIVE YEARS OF REASONS TO RESIST
CORPORATE GLOBALIZATION
Lori Wallach and Michelle Sforza
Introduction by Ralph Nader
80 pages / $5.95 / ISBN: 1-58322-035-6

THE CASE OF MUMIA ABU-JAMAL:
A LIFE IN THE BALANCE
Amnesty International
64 pages / $6.95 / ISBN: 1-58322-081-X

WEAPONS IN SPACE
Karl Grossman
80 pages / $6.95 / ISBN: 1-58322-044-5

10 REASONS TO ABOLISH THE IMF & WORLD BANK
Kevin Dahaner
104 pages / $6.95 / ISBN: 1-58322-464-5

SENT BY EARTH
Alice Walker
64 pages / $5.00 / ISBN: 1-58322-491-2

TERRORISM: THEIRS AND OURS
Eqbal Ahmad
64 pages / $6.95 / ISBN: 1-58322-490-4

OPEN MEDIA BOOKS

9-11
Noam Chomsky
128 pages / $8.95 / ISBN: 1-58322-489-0

TERRORISM AND WAR
Howard Zinn
160 pages / $9.95 / ISBN: 1-58322-493-9

BIN LADEN, ISLAM, AND AMERICA'S NEW "WAR ON TERRORISM"
As`ad AbuKhalil
112 pages / $8.95 / ISBN: 1-58322-492-0

TO ORDER ADDITIONAL SERIES TITLES CALL 1 (800) 596-7437

OR VISIT WWW.SEVENSTORIES.COM

THE OPEN MEDIA PAMPHLET SERIES

SECRET TRIALS AND EXECUTIONS

Military Tribunals and the Threat to Democracy

BARBARA OLSHANSKY

AND THE CENTER FOR CONSTITUTIONAL RIGHTS

Series editor Greg Ruggiero

SEVEN STORIES PRESS / NEW YORK

This book is dedicated to Craig Acorn,
my comrade, friend, and love.
—BARBARA OLSHANSKY

Copyright © 2002 by Barbara Olshansky and the Center
for Constitutional Rights

A Seven Stories Press First Edition,
published in association with Open Media.

All rights reserved. No part of this book may
be reproduced, stored in a retrieval system, or transmitted in
any form, by any means, including mechanical, electric, pho-
tocopying, recording or otherwise, without the prior written
permission of the publisher.

ISBN: 1-58322-537-4

9 8 7 6 5 4 3 2 1

Cover design by Greg Ruggiero.

Cover photos: U.S. Department of Defense photos of
"detainees" at the U.S.-controlled Camp X-Ray,
Guantanamo Bay, Cuba, January 2002.

Printed in Canada.

CONTENTS

Since the attacks of September 11, the United States has witnessed a sweeping revision of its immigration laws, foreign intelligence gathering operations, and domestic law enforcement procedures. These changes, like those adopted during some of the most notorious episodes in our nation's history, involve a profound curtailment of our civil liberties. In the not-too-distant past, the U.S. government reacted to national security threats with policies that we now remember with horror. The Red Scare and the Palmer Raids after the First World War, the internment of Japanese Americans during the Second World War, the repressive and chilling measures of the McCarthy era, and the harassment and prosecution of political dissidents during and after the Vietnam War all represent policies that history will forever recall with regret and shame. Given this unfortunate past, we need to closely examine the current Administration's responses to September 11 and assess what those responses mean in terms of international law, the U.S. Constitution, and our commitment to democracy. We must take a thorough look at what the Bush administration is doing in the name of defending national security and ask ourselves: Is such a compromise of civil liberties, democracy, and human rights ever tolerable?

I

A MILITARY ORDER IS SIGNED

Declaring an "extraordinary emergency," on November 13, 2001, President George W. Bush signed an unprecedented order authorizing the creation of special military tribunals to try non-citizens suspected of terrorism.[1] While these tribunals or commissions may take place either inside or outside the United States, all such trials will be almost entirely outside of the cardinal constitutional guarantees embodied in the American criminal justice system. With a single swipe of his pen, President Bush replaced the democratic pillars of our legal system with that of a military commission system in which he, or his designee, is rule-maker, investigator, accuser, prosecutor, judge, jury, sentencing court, reviewing court, and jailer or executioner. This new system radically abandons the core constitutional guarantees at the heart of American democracy: the rights to an independent judiciary, trial by jury, public proceedings, due process, and appeals to higher courts. In the newly authorized military tribunal system, all of these safeguards against injustice are gone.

At the time the November 13 Military Order was signed, the United States Department of Justice had already detained more than 1,200 immigrants as part of its initial investigation, and was in the process of authorizing local law enforcement agencies across the country to question 5,000 young men of Middle Eastern descent who had entered the country legally after January 1, 2000. While this roundup was purportedly part of a Department of Justice effort to investigate the workings of the Al Qaeda network— the group believed to be responsible for the September 11 attacks—the questionnaire sent to the 5,000 young men actually sought general information about each individual's political associations. Although the Department of Justice readily admits that its actions constitute racial/ethnic profiling, it nevertheless insists that such measures are necessary to the criminal investigation no matter how broadly the net is cast.[2]

The Military Order and the detention and questioning of people of Middle Eastern descent came on the heels of the Department of Justice's decision on October 30, 2001, to authorize governmental monitoring of attorney-client communications between an individual detained by the federal government and his lawyer when the U.S. Attorney General believes that intercepting the communication may be helpful in deterring acts of violence or terrorism.[3] This unprecedented intrusion on the previously sacrosanct

8

attorney-client privilege permits eavesdropping on conversations between lawyers and their clients without prior judicial approval, regardless of whether anyone has been charged with a crime. The Attorney General's unilateral determination that a "reasonable suspicion" exists is all that is now needed to justify such monitoring. The new policy has been widely criticized because of its chilling effect on attorney-client communications, its impairment of the attorney-client privilege, and its subversion of the Sixth Amendment's guarantee of effective assistance of counsel in criminal cases.[4]

These new policies constitute only a small piece of what is quickly becoming one of the most sweeping and sustained governmental efforts to investigate and prosecute "enemies" since the McCarthy era. The implications of such changes are so far-reaching and antithetical to our most basic democratic principles that immediate public scrutiny and debate are needed to assess the degree to which the new policies may be in violation of the U.S. Constitution and international agreements on basic human rights. The creation of these broad investigatory, adjudicatory, and sentencing powers are going to exact a staggering price in terms of our constitutional rights and freedoms, yet the Bush Administration maintains that such sacrifices are needed to counter the new security risks posed by terrorism.[5] A broad range of citizens, policymakers, educators, lawyers, and civil rights activists, however, have expressed their grave concerns about the toll these measures will also take on our democratic institu-

tions, our credibility in the international community, and our ability to defend and advance human
rights around the world. Could this possibly be a toll
that Americans are willing to pay?

II

TO WHOM DOES THE MILITARY ORDER APPLY AND WHAT TYPES OF TRIALS DOES IT PERMIT?

To provide a framework for this analysis, this pamphlet looks at the history of the few instances in which this country has employed military tribunals; whether the current situation warrants invocation of the type of forum proposed by the President; the official positions that our government has taken regarding the use of military tribunals by other nations; the legal basis for the specific form of military tribunal that is established by the Military Order; what alternatives exist to bring to justice those who may be guilty of terrorist acts; what constitutional principles are at stake in this decision; and how the decision to use military tribunals may impact America's credibility and moral authority in the community. The Military Order gives the President the power to:

- Identify the particular persons who will be tried by military commission [commissions?];
- Create the rules under which the commissions will operate and change them at will;
- Appoint the judges, prosecutors, and defense lawyers;
- Decide the sentence upon conviction;
- Decide all appeals; and
- Conduct the entire process, including executions in secret, without any accountability to Congress, the courts, or the American public.

In these ways, the Order provides the President and, in some instances, the Secretary of Defense with the greatest array of legal powers to be exercised in the justice system that has ever been vested in a single person, office, or branch of government since the birth of this nation. In fact, the Order is stunning in its abandonment of the doctrine of Separation of Powers and in its forsaking of cherished constitutional principles.

WHAT ARE THE RULES FOR THE MILITARY COMMISSIONS?

On March 21, 2002, as authorized by the Military Order, Secretary of Defense Donald H. Rumsfeld issued Military Commission Order No. 1 (the "Commission Rules") establishing guidelines for conducting military commissions pursuant to the President's November 13 Order.[6] While the Commission Rules prescribe certain procedures for commission trials, the language of these Defense Department guidelines makes clear that such procedures are subject to change *at any time* by either the President or the Secretary of Defense.[7]

Not only are the protections provided by the Commission Rules subject to change indefinitely, they are unenforceable and are therefore only available to the accused individual at the discretion of the President, the Secretary of Defense as his designee, or the appointed commission members. This fact is made abundantly clear by the language of the Rules themselves. Section 10 states that the Rules do not create any rights that are enforceable by anyone against the United States, its agencies, officers or employees. This language prevents anyone from bringing a lawsuit—or raising any claim—that a military commission did not comply with its own governing rules. By eliminating all bases upon which a person may seek to enforce the Rules, the Secretary of Defense has conveyed to all who might be compelled to participate in such proceedings that compliance will not be policed in any significant or publicly accountable way. In sum, to the extent that the Commission Rules provide any protection at all for those who may be charged and tried under the Military Order, that protection is both unstable and ultimately unenforceable.

WHO IS COVERED BY THE MILITARY ORDER? The Military Order leaves to the President alone the decision of who will be brought before the military tribunals. Under the Order, the "non-citizens" prosecuted by military tribunals will be those people that the President has "reason to believe":

(1) are members of Al Qaeda;
(2) are in any way involved in "acts of international terrorism;" *or*
(3) have "knowingly harbored" persons falling within either of the first two categories.[8]

The Military Order covers non-U.S. citizens, a term that, literally read, includes legal permanent residents of this country as well as people who may be entitled to citizenship status but have not yet been officially granted that status.[9] Additionally, while the Order states that it applies only to individuals who are non-citizens, nowhere does it specify what will happen in those cases in which the question of citizenship status is in doubt, as it may be for people who have applied for political asylum. The discretion to decide this issue is also vested solely in the President.[10]

The Administration's effort to defend the Military Order's elimination of constitutional rights on the ground that the Order does not apply to U.S. citizens is deeply troubling. This country has never accepted the principle that only citizens are entitled to the benefits of our constitutional guarantees when they are subject to criminal prosecution.[11] In fact, the United States Supreme Court has held steadfast to this deeply rooted principle of equal protection under the Bill of Rights even in those periods in which the country sought to impose harsh measures to address threats to national security. For example, more than a century ago Congress enacted a racist and xenophobic statute that subjected Chi-

BARBARA OLSHANSKY

nese immigrants caught without proper documents to one year of hard labor without providing them with a criminal trial complete with all of the guarantees of the Bill of Rights. On appeal to the Supreme Court in *Wong Wing v. United States*, 163 U.S. 228 (1896), the Court struck down the statute finding that it was an unlawful deprivation of the immigrants' constitutional rights. The Supreme Court again emphasized our Constitution's commitment to this key democratic principle in 2001, when it held in *Zadvydas v. Davis*, 121 S. Ct. 2491, 2500 (2001), that "the Due Process Clause applies to all 'persons' within the United States, including aliens, whether their presence here is lawful, unlawful, temporary, or permanent."

The Military Order's disavowal of our core constitutional rules is even more disturbing when we look at just how wide a net it casts. A quick look at the three categories of "non-citizens" covered by the Order shows that, even though the Administration painted the Order as an effort to address the limited situation in which Al Qaeda leaders might be captured and held for trial, two of the three categories set forth do not mention Al Qaeda at all and instead aim at a much broader group of immigrants.[12] For example, people charged with "aiding" or simply "harboring" other persons who are subject to the Order—i.e., people who have committed a *civilian criminal act and not a military-like terrorist act*—may be tried by a military tribunal under the third category set forth in the Order.[13]

The second category of those covered by the Order

is vague and ambiguous, and therefore extremely broad as well. The Order contains no definition of the term "international terrorism," and leaves entirely up to the President the determination of the type of conduct that will be held to violate the law and subject an individual to prosecution by military commission. Unlike our criminal justice system, in which the prosecution tries people for violating specific criminal laws that have been written and adopted by either our state legislatures or by Congress, under the Military Order, the President *alone* decides what types of acts having "an adverse effect on the United States, its citizens, national security, foreign policy, or economy" will be punishable as "international terrorism."[14]

The range of lawful activities that could be targeted by this undefined and extremely broad category of offenses is staggering. In the absence of any definition of the offense of "international terrorism," the potential for conveniently changing the rules to include different conduct as new circumstances arise is immense, as is the potential for the use of military commissions to serve ends other than the furtherance of justice. Even if the phrase "international terrorism" were to be defined in terms of its use in existing laws, the concerns raised above would not diminish.[15] Under the Anti-Terrorism and Effective Death Penalty Act of 1996, "terrorism" is defined as the use of any force or violence to achieve a political aim. The use of such a definition here would mean that persons engaging in lawful, nonviolent political activities—such as civil disobedience protests—that result in minor property damage or any measure of physical inter-action with police officers could be subjected to trial by a military commission.

Similarly, because the federal criminal code now prohibits providing material support to organizations with connections to terrorists, regardless of whether that support actually furthers any terrorist activity, people who, for example, provide money for human-itarian medical assistance to an organization allegedly linked to a terrorist group may be "detained" and prosecuted by military commission even if they are unaware of the link.[16] Given these circumstances, the risk that the Military Order will ensnare innocent people seeking to help relief efforts in other nations seems very high indeed.

In addition to the vague, ambiguous, and broad def-initions of who may be covered, the tentacles of the Order also reach out broadly by means of another mechanism. The Military Order simply states that the people who will be prosecuted under the Order are those whom the President "determine[s] from time to time in writing that...there is *reason to believe* that such individual, at the relevant times, is or was a member of the organization known as Al Qaeda...."[17] Although aimed at reaching members of Al Qaeda, this provision raises serious concerns as well. First, the language tells us that the decision of who to pros-ecute by military tribunal will be based entirely on the President's *subjective assessment* and not upon the more stringent and objective standard of "proba-ble cause to believe that a crime has been committed" as required by the Supreme Court's decisions interpreting the constitutional boundaries of our criminal laws. Second, this part of the Order vests the discretion of who to charge solely in the President, and does not require any further corroboration or additional evidence before the military commission process is invoked. The lack of any judicial review at this stage of the process—the charging stage—means that the President will *not* be called upon to explain why he has "reason to believe" someone falls within one of the three categories, nor to specify what proof he has gathered in support of his determination. This circumvention of judicial review plainly contradicts settled constitutional law.[18]

Finally, because there is no time frame governing the President's determination of who is to be charged and tried by military commission, a person who, for example, provided housing many years ago to an individual now suspected of being a terrorist could get dragged into the black hole of the military commission.

WHAT TYPES OF OFFENSES ARE COVERED BY THE MILITARY ORDER?

As noted above, the Military Order's lack of any definition for the term "international terrorism" means that the President alone will determine the type of conduct that will be held to violate the law.[19]

The absence of any provisions in the Military Order mandating that the President specify precisely which acts qualify as "international terrorism" and the lack of any specification of offenses in the Commission Rules means that no one will be able to

BARBARA OLSHANSKY

ascertain exactly what is forbidden, and thus what behavior is to be avoided. In this country, no criminal law that sought to punish a person on the basis of such vague and ambiguous terms would ever pass muster under our Constitution. Our Supreme Court has long adhered to the principle that within the meaning of the Due Process Clause of the Fourteenth Amendment a law is unconstitutional if it is so ambiguous that a person of common understanding cannot know what conduct is forbidden.[20]

Furthermore, in the absence of definitions establishing the elements of covered offenses, we cannot gauge whether individuals brought before the military commissions are being treated equally in terms of the offenses they are charged with, the type of evidence that is used against them, or the rulings made in their individual cases. We have no means of ensuring consistency in the charging, trying, convicting, or sentencing of those persons brought before the military commissions. Free of democratic accountability and invested with the power to order executions in secret, the President and the Secretary of Defense have granted these commissions totalitarian powers.

The Military Order also appears to extend the jurisdiction of the military commissions beyond trials concerning "violations of the laws of war" to those concerning violations of all "other applicable laws."[21] This broad phrase could be easily invoked by the executive branch to use military commissions to try people accused of committing state and federal crimes that have no relationship whatsoever to any terrorist activity. The Order thus appears to permit governmental prosecutions for common crimes in which our civilian criminal justice system with all of its constitutional guarantees is completely bypassed. No justification is given for this exemption of state and federal common criminal cases from our criminal justice system.[22] Nor has any explanation been offered by the Administration as to why all immigrants are to be denied their basic fundamental rights when they are not even being charged with participating in or supporting terrorist activities or groups. By including this provision in the Military Order, the Administration has plainly stated its position: All non-citizens, regardless of their affiliations or activities, are viewed with suspicion, and may be denied—at the sole discretion of the President—the constitutional protections that we have *always afforded to every person* accused of a crime in this country. Our commitment to equal treatment has been undermined without so much as a nod to congressional enactments, judicial precedent, or public opinion.

All of this means that the Military Order authorizes the President to determine who will receive the traditional constitutional protections of the federal courts and who will be remanded to the secret proceedings of a military commission. These powers— powers that are constitutionally vested first in the legislatures to define and codify criminal laws, and then in the courts to determine the parameters of their own jurisdiction and to try those accused of violating the laws—have been grabbed away from the legislative and judicial branches of government, and housed solely in the person of the President. Our legal system has never sanctioned the authorization of such unfettered power in any single branch of government, let alone in a single official. Such a drastic change radically violates the core principles of the Constitution, principles that qualify this country to be a genuine democracy.

HOW WILL THE TRIALS HELD BY THE MILITARY COMMISSIONS BE CONDUCTED?

In addition to the lack of definitions for the different offenses that will subject someone to trial by military commission, the Military Order contains little information regarding the specific rules of conduct for the commissions themselves; it simply states that prisoners must be treated "humanely"[23] and must be given "a full and fair trial" without defining these terms.[24] However, the Order does specify that the rules of procedure for commissions are to be determined by the Secretary of Defense.[25] In this way, too, the executive branch has assumed the judicial role of determining the scope of the constitutional protections to be afforded the accused.[26]

THE MILITARY ORDER PERMITS UNLIMITED AND UNAPPEALABLE PRE-TRIAL DETENTION Even a basic examination of the Military Order and the Commission Rules reveals that the President has cast aside many basic rights and guarantees in the name of expediency.[27] The guidelines set forth in the Order and the Commission Rules indicate that few—if any—of the due process safeguards for which our justice system is renowned will be provided.

For example, the Order makes clear in two separate provisions that the Secretary of Defense has the complete authority to determine the conditions of detention of the individuals who are charged under the Order.[28] These provisions give the Secretary license to detain individuals *indefinitely* in direct violation of even the most recent congressional enactment addressing this issue, the USA PATRIOT Act of October 26, 2001. They also give the Secretary the authority to specify the place of detention *anywhere in the world.* The USA PATRIOT Act requires that non-citizens who are detained by the government be charged with a crime or immigration violation within seven days of their detention.[29] It then permits judicial review of the basis for the detention through the mechanism of a petition for *habeas corpus* seeking release from custody. In contrast, no time limitations apply under the military order for informing those detained of the charges against them, nor do any avenues of judicial review exist for those being held. By means of the Military Order, then, the President has accomplished precisely those objectives which Congress would not accept when it considered the Administration's proposal on the USA PATRIOT Act. Apparently, the Administration has used the Military Order to circumvent the considered determination of Congress on this precise issue.

THE MILITARY ORDER CASTS ASIDE MANY KEY FOURTH, FIFTH, AND SIXTH AMENDMENT RIGHTS

THE IMPACT ON FOURTH AMENDMENT RIGHTS

Both the subjective basis for detention and the

unlimited restraint of the accused permitted by the Military Order constitute undeniable violations of our Fourth Amendment guarantee against unreasonable searches and seizures.[30] The longstanding protection afforded every accused person by the Fourth Amendment requirement that there be probable cause to arrest has been dissolved by this Presidential decree.[31] Similarly eliminated is the Fourth Amendment protection against prolonged detention without a hearing before a judicial officer to determine whether probable cause for arrest exists.[32]

In addition to these unlimited restraints on one's liberty, the Military Order makes clear that other fundamental principles of our justice system—principles aimed at ensuring the veracity of the evidence presented and relied upon in convictions—are not applicable to military commissions. Under the Order and the Commission Rules, all evidence deemed to have "probative value to a reasonable person" may be used in the proceedings.[33] This means that hearsay and other evidence that our federal courts have determined is unreliable or illegally obtained—such as testimony resulting from coerced confessions, unsworn statements, and unauthenticated reports—may now be used.[34] No longer will the Fourth Amendment's guarantee against unreasonable searches and seizures or its prohibition against the use of evidence gathered in violation of this guarantee protect us and our homes against invasions of privacy and violations of security.

THE IMPACT ON FIFTH AMENDMENT RIGHTS

While the Commission Rules state that the

accused "shall not be required to testify during trial," the Rules expressly *permit* the use of pretrial statements made by the accused regardless of the circumstances under which such statements were made.[35] This license to permit the use of compelled statements and hearsay means that the Fifth Amendment's guarantee against compelled self-incrimination will no longer protect individuals suspected of wrongdoing from psychological and physical tactics—which, when used by foreign governments and groups, the U.S. condemns—meant to extract "confessions" regardless of their truth.[36] The heart of our justice system is that it affords protection not just to the accused, but to the search for truth itself. Can we still call this country a democracy if we are willing to relinquish our constitutional rights and breach international standards of basic human rights in the pursuit of punishing suspected enemies?

The Fifth Amendment's due process guarantees suffer additional blows under the Order through the structure and staffing of the military commissions. While in a traditional criminal trial the judge is entirely independent of the prosecutor and sits by virtue of an appointment from the judicial branch as opposed to the executive branch, *all* of the key roles in the military commission process are to be filled by military officers acting upon designation by the President. The evidence will be presented by military officers acting as prosecutors and will be weighed by military officers acting as judges, all of whom report through the chain of command to the President in his role as Commander-in-Chief.[37]

Even "detailed" defense counsel-the attorney who will work under the guidance of the Chief Defense Counsel-will be a military officer. Although the Commission Rules permit the accused to retain his own civilian defense attorney, that attorney must first be found eligible for access to information classified as "Secret" under Defense Department guidelines.[38] Furthermore, even if the privately retained civilian attorney meets these requirements and is permitted to participate in the proceeding, the appointed military detailed defense counsel remains in charge of the defense, and may not be dismissed by the accused. In addition, the Rules state that the civilian defense counsel— even if he or she has Secret level clearance— will not be permitted to be present during any portion of the commission proceeding that is ordered closed by the Presiding Officer or the President.[39] In this manner, the military commissions-staffed and controlled by military officers who work directly at the behest of the President-abandon and offend the Constitution's due process guarantee of an independent judiciary.

Another disturbing aspect of the Military Order is that double jeopardy—the constitutional principle anchored in the Fifth Amendment that the same sovereign cannot try a person twice for the same offense—is never mentioned. The fundamental guarantee against double jeopardy encompasses several protections: It protects against a second prosecution for the same offense after one is acquitted; it protects against a second prosecution for the same offense after one is convicted; and it protects against the imposition of multiple punishments for the same offense.[40]

Because the guarantees of the Fifth Amendment's double jeopardy clause are limited—for example, they do not apply in a number of different types of proceedings that may result in penalties—the omission of any reference to this constitutional guarantee leaves open the possibility that an individual may be charged and tried in the civilian federal court, acquitted, and then detained and brought to trial before a military commission for the same offense. Indeed, the Order seems designed to permit the executive branch to try its hand first in the federal courts, and if it seems that this prosecution may be unsuccessful, bring precisely the same case before a military commission where it will be permitted to use evidence that would be inadmissible in the federal court case (because, perhaps, it was tainted by an illegal search, force, or coercion), thereby providing a better chance of conviction. Plainly, the Order places no constraint whatsoever on the President or the Secretary of Defense should they decide to seek a second bite at the apple.

THE IMPACT ON SIXTH AMENDMENT RIGHTS

Many of our Sixth Amendment guarantees are trampled by the Military Order as well.[41] The Sixth Amendment provides for the defendant in a criminal case to be afforded a speedy and public trial; to have the benefit of an impartial jury selected from the area where the crime occurred; to be informed of the accusations against him; to confront the witnesses against

BARBARA OLSHANSKY

him; to be able to use compulsory process to obtain favorable witnesses; and to have the assistance of counsel in presenting his case. But the Military Order and the Commission Rules make clear that there is no right to a jury trial; those accused under the Order will be tried before three to seven members of the U.S. armed forces. The primary purpose of this cardinal constitutional guarantee—one deemed "fundamental to the American scheme of justice" by the Supreme Court—is to protect against government oppression by allowing members of the community to participate in the determination of guilt or innocence. As the Supreme Court has emphasized, the right to a jury trial gives the person accused "an inestimable safeguard against the corrupt or overzealous prosecutor and against the compliant, biased or eccentric judge."[42] Why have we eliminated a safeguard that lies at the heart of our system of justice?

Despite proclamations to the contrary, the President's military commission system does *not* provide for the right to a public trial. In fact, the Commission Rules expressly state that the proceedings will be held open entirely *at the discretion* of the President or the Secretary of Defense as his designee or that of the Presiding Officer.[43] The Rules also provide that a request to close the proceedings may be made to the Presiding Officer in chambers without the attendance of defense counsel, and may include a request to specifically exclude civilian defense counsel and the accused from the proceedings.[44] In addition, the grounds for closing the proceedings spelled out in the Rules are so broad that the discretion is virtually unfettered: the protection of classified information; the protection of unspecified information that may not be disclosed for other reasons; the possible revelation of intelligence and law enforcement methods or activities; and other undefined national security interests. Given the objectives of the military commissions and the breadth of the grounds for closure, it seems very likely that nearly all such proceedings will be closed. Like the right to a jury trial, the guarantee of a public trial stands as a bulwark against the use of courts as instruments of persecution. However, it also serves other significant functions in a democracy: It provides the public with the opportunity to assess the government's actions and thereby ensures accountability; it inspires confidence in the basic fairness of the judicial system; and it vindicates the concerns of the victims and the community that the offenders be held accountable for their criminal actions. These important policies are thoroughly swept away by the closure of commission proceedings.

Also fatally compromised by the secrecy of the commission proceedings are the Sixth Amendment guarantees that the accused be permitted to confront the witnesses and evidence against him. The Supreme Court has held that this is a "fundamental right" that is "essential to a fair trial."[45] Nevertheless, the Commission Rules adopted by the Secretary of Defense appear to thwart the exercise of this right at every turn. For example, although the prosecution is required to notify the person accused of the charges against him at the beginning of the commission proceedings, the Rules do not specify any minimum time prior to the trial in which this must occur. Nor do the Rules even require that the charges be presented in a language that the accused understands.[46] Indeed, the provision of an interpreter is far from guaranteed in commission proceedings; the Rules state only that the President or the Defense Secretary "may appoint one or more interpreters to assist the Defense, *as necessary*."[47] Furthermore, because of the provisions of the Military Order prohibiting disclosure of classified information, together with the provisions of the Commission Rules permitting the closure of the proceedings and the exclusion of the accused, those who are detained pursuant to the Order might never be able to see the evidence against them.[48] Under such rules, it is the defense—not justice—that is blind.

THE MILITARY ORDER ERASES THE CONSTITUTIONAL GUARANTEE OF *HABEAS CORPUS* The Military Order's evisceration of an accused person's right to judicial review of the decision of a military commission also affronts democratic principles. The Order grants military commissions "exclusive jurisdiction" over the covered offenses such that individuals subject to the Order "shall not be privileged to seek any remedy or maintain any proceeding" in "any court of the United States," "any foreign nation," or "any international tribunal."[49] The Order is clearly intended to eliminate all judicial review of the process, including the "privilege of *habeas corpus*," a fundamental constitutional right.[50] The writ of *habeas corpus* is the means by which a prisoner seeks judicial review of the bases for his detention or imprisonment and involves the presentation of constitutional challenges.

The bedrock principle of our justice system is that government may not deprive a person of his or her liberty without due process of law. The Supreme Court has long held, beginning in the nineteenth century and continuing *without* exception to the present day, that all "persons" within the jurisdiction of the United States are entitled to the protections of the due process clause.[51] In fact, even during World War II, the writ of *habeas corpus* was available to members of the German and Japanese militaries so that they could test the authority of a military commission to detain and try them.[52]

The writ of *habeas corpus* is one of the primary constitutional mechanisms intended to provide those incarcerated with due process protections against arbitrary, biased, and unlawful detention. Chief Justice Rehnquist has said that this privilege "has been rightly regarded as a safeguard against executive tyranny, and an essential safeguard to individual liberty."[53] The language of the Constitution makes clear that only Congress, not the President, may suspend the writ of *habeas corpus*, and even then this power is restricted to cases of actual rebellion or invasion.[54] In fact, such an extreme measure has not been used since the Civil War. Nevertheless, the Military Order suspends the writ. Under the Order, a person may be detained indefinitely without being charged or brought to trial; convictions and sentences by a military commission, including "life imprisonment or death," can be reviewed only by the same officials who made the initial determination to charge the person accused: the President or the Secretary of Defense.

The sources cited by the Administration as authority for issuing the Military Order do not support the suspension of the writ of *habeas corpus*. The Congressional Resolution Authorizing the Use of Military Force makes no reference whatsoever to arrest, detention, trial, appeal, judicial review, or *habeas corpus* relief. Similarly, nothing in either Section 821 or Section 836 of the Uniform Code of Military Justice provides the basis for congressional suspension of the writ.

Not only is there no legal authority supporting the Administration's position, there *is* ample evidence that Congress did *not* intend for the writ of *habeas corpus* to be suspended under the present circumstances. When Congress passed the USA PATRIOT Act, it plainly intended, as the full name of the Act implies, to create a *comprehensive* set of tools for the federal government to use in its intelligence gathering and law enforcement efforts to combat terrorism.[55] Accordingly, Congress specifically contemplated and addressed the issue of the availability of the writ of *habeas corpus* in Section 412 of the USA PATRIOT Act entitled "Mandatory Detention of Suspected Terrorists; *Habeas Corpus*; Judicial Review." Section 412 amends a provision of the Immigration and Nationality Act (INA) to require that the government, when it detains immigrants subject to the INA, either criminally charge them or place them in removal proceedings within seven days of the start of their detention unless their release would threaten the national security of the United States. If the Attorney General believes that there would be such a danger, he must issue a certification to that effect, and must recertify his findings every six months that the individual remains in detention.[56] This section of the USA PATRIOT Act also provides for *habeas corpus* proceedings to review the government's decisions regarding detention: The individual may apply for such relief from the Supreme Court, any Justice of the Supreme Court, any circuit judge of the D.C. Circuit Court of Appeals, or any district court with jurisdiction.[57] While Section 412 of the USA PATRIOT Act codifies congressional intent to ensure the availability of the writ of *habeas corpus*, the Military Order provides for no release process, no right to a petition for a writ of *habeas corpus*, and no right to appeal any decision made by the executive branch from detention through conviction and sentencing. Congress's action on the subject of *habeas corpus* is clear; the USA PATRIOT Act preserves the writ. The President's Military Order not only seeks to exercise a power that is constitutionally reserved to Congress, but also seeks to undermine Congress's specific exercise of its power. There can be no more blatant and profound example of unlawful Presidential overreaching, of conduct taken in contravention to the expressed will of Congress, than in this instance.[58]

THE MILITARY ORDER CREATES A SYSTEM IN WHICH BOTH SECRET TRI-ALS AND EXECUTIONS ARE AUTHORIZED The Military Order and the Commission Rules expressly authorize the "closure" of a military commission's proceedings, permitting the President and the Secretary of Defense to conduct secret proceedings should they so choose. In this way, the Military Order creates a system that answers only to the President. Under this new system, individuals can be arrested, detained indefinitely without being charged, tried in secret before a military panel on evidence that may not be examined or tested, convicted by a two-thirds vote, sentenced to death, and executed without Congress, the judiciary, or the American public ever knowing anything about any aspect of the proceedings. Thus, under President Bush's new Military Order, the checks and balances that define democracy are eliminated, public knowledge is censored, and the President, free from accountability, is invested with totalitarian power. Never before has the American public been forced to shut its eyes, stop its ears, and close its mouth when the pursuit of justice was at stake.

Yet even more disturbing is the fact that the Military Order gives the President complete authority to reach whatever "final decision" he considers proper.[59] The Order provides for no constraint on the President's decision-making in this regard; it may therefore be construed as permitting the President to issue a final decision that ignores the findings and penalties imposed by the military commission. The only constraint placed on the executive branch by the Commission Rules is that a finding of "not guilty" may not be changed to a finding of "guilty."[60] However, the President could order a new trial under the *same or more serious charges* or impose a much stiffer sentence than that of the commission. The vesting of such authority in the President is so utterly inconsistent with the bedrock principles of American democracy that no argument can be made in support of such a grant of power.

While at first glance the Commission Rules appear to address some of these issues, upon closer examination it becomes clear that those sections of the Rules seemingly intended to address public criticism do not achieve this end. The problem lies in the fact that Section 7(B) of the Commission Rules expressly states that, in the event of a conflict between the requirements of the Military Order and the Commission Rules (or any supplementary regulations subsequently issued), the provisions of the Military Order govern. Under this rule, Section 6(F) of the Commission Rules, which provides that a sentence of death may only be reached by a "unanimous vote of all of the members" of the commission, is *overruled* by Section 4(b)(7) of the Military Order, which states that sentencing only requires the "concurrence of two-thirds of the members of the commission." Even if the Rules were intended to repair this flaw in the Order, the provision permitting the imposition of a death sentence without even a unanimous vote stands.

THE MILITARY ORDER CREATES A SIGNIFICANT RISK OF CONVICTION AND EXECUTION OF THE INNOCENT With the overt goal of expediency, and the covert objective of vengeance, the Military Order deliberately sacrifices those constitutional protections that are intended to prevent the conviction and punishment of the innocent. The guarantees of public trial by jury or an independent and impartial judge, evidentiary rules, the privilege against self-incrimination, defense counsel of one's choice, and the right to appeal are all intended to ensure that the process is fair, just, and truth-seeking. Why should we tolerate the government's abandoning of these principles now, when our justice system has successfully prosecuted terrorists while complying with these principles in the past? How can we permit the subversion of these basic democratic values when their loss may adversely affect not only the welfare of immigrants accused of crimes unrelated to terrorism but all of us? How can sacrificing rules that safeguard the innocent be deemed morally acceptable when the possible consequences include life imprisonment or execution?

III

WHAT ARE THE LEGAL AND HISTORICAL GROUNDS FOR THE MILITARY COMMISSIONS CREATED BY THE PRESIDENT'S ORDER?

According to the Bush Administration, the Military Order is constitutional, politically necessary, and morally appropriate. The Administration points to three sources of federal authority for the Order:

➤ The President's constitutional authority as Commander-in-Chief of the Armed Forces of the United States;[61]
➤ The Congressional Joint Resolution Authorizing the Use of Military Force;[62] and
➤ Two provisions of the Uniform Code of Military Justice (UCMJ).[63]

Not one of these sources, however, grants the President the authority that he now claims.

DOES THE PRESIDENT HAVE THE LEGAL AUTHORITY TO CREATE MILITARY COMMISSIONS TO TRY TERRORISTS?

Neither the Constitution nor any federal statute permits the President to create a military court with the authority to try all cases of alleged international terrorism against the United States. The Constitution contains no article, section, or clause that provides the President with the power to create military commissions, and the Supreme Court has never held that the President has any implied authority to do so absent congressional action. In fact, the Constitution is quite clear that when Congress acts, it *alone* has the authority to create and permit the use of military commissions. This authority is created by the powers vested in Congress to "constitute tribunals inferior to the Supreme Court,"[64] "to define and punish... Offenses against the Law of Nations,"[65] and "to make rules for the government and regulation of the land and naval forces."[66] The Military Order, in direct contravention of the separation of powers principle of our government, lodges these powers in the Secretary of Defense, acting at the direction of the President, without congressional approval.

The Joint Resolution Authorizing the Use of Military Force cannot provide the President with the power he seeks to exercise here. The Joint Resolution permits the President to use "all necessary and appropriate force against those nations, organizations, or persons" that were involved in the attacks on September 11 "in order to prevent future actions of international ter-

rorism against the United States" by them.[67] It authorizes the President to activate the reserves and send
troops to Afghanistan, but says nothing about the
methods to be used to try those who are captured and
accused of participating in the attacks.[68]

The third source of authority cited by the Administration also provides no support for the Military
Order. Neither Section 821 nor Section 836 of the
Uniform Code of Military Justice authorizes the use
of secret military tribunals by any agency or branch
of government. Section 821 merely states that *if and
when* military commissions are properly authorized
"by statute or by the law of war" the existence of
courts-martial will not deprive such commissions of
their ability to hear a case.[69] This section therefore
addresses only those specific situations involving
offenders and offenses that are traditionally tried
under the law of war by military commissions, it cannot authorize the *creation* of military commissions.

Similarly, while Section 836 delegates to the President the authority to delineate rules of evidence and
procedure for courts-martial and military commissions, it does not authorize him to create military
commissions.[70] Furthermore, the limitations placed
upon the President's power to prescribe the procedures undermines the Administration's claim that
Section 36 gives the President the broad authority he
has assumed under the Military Order. Section 36
states that the procedures created "may not be contrary to or inconsistent with [the UCMJ]." However,
the framework of the Military Order is entirely
inconsistent with the due process requirements spec-

BARBARA OLSHANSKY

ified in the UCMJ. For example, unlike the Military Order, the UCMJ gives the defendant the right to choose counsel, gives the defense a role in the selection of the court-martial panel, requires unanimity in applying a death sentence, and provides for appellate review of decisions.[71] Given these inconsistencies, the Military Order would be egregiously defective even if Section 36 did provide the authority for the Order.[72]

WHAT IS THE HISTORICAL PRECEDENT FOR THE MILITARY ORDER? HAVE WE DONE THIS BEFORE?

America's use of military commissions in the past provides no support whatsoever for the use of the military commissions presently authorized by the Military Order.

As historical support for its position, the Administration has pointed to a World War II decision by the Supreme Court, *Ex parte Quirn*, 317 U.S. 1 (1942), in which the Court upheld the propriety of a trial of eight German saboteurs by military commission.[73] However, that decision does not support the Administration's position. At the time of *Ex parte Quirn*, Congress had issued a formal declaration of war and had expressly authorized the trial by military commission of "enemy aliens" who violate the law of war—i.e., citizens of a state with which the United States is at war—in two statutes, Articles 81 and 82 of the Articles of War.[74] In *Ex parte Quirn*, the Supreme Court based its conclusion on the international law of war as it existed at the time, and upheld the authority of the military commission to try enemy-state combatants for their unlawful actions within the United States during a *declared* international armed conflict.

The circumstances under which the Court decided that case, however, are not present today. None of the proposed defendants in the current circumstances are likely to be charged with violations of the law of war committed in the context of a declared armed conflict. Congress has not made a formal declaration of war, nor are the members of Al Qaeda "enemy aliens" within the meaning of international law; they are not combatants or soldiers from an enemy state's army.[75]

International treaty law defines the specific circumstances in which the "laws of war" apply. These rules have been accepted and adopted by the United States.[76] Under the Geneva Conventions, a state of war exists only when a conflict arises between nation-states.[77] While the Geneva Conventions also spell out rules of war that apply for "non-international armed conflicts" or non-country conflicts, they clearly provide that such rules apply only to conflicts between a state's armed forces and dissident groups within that state that are under responsible command and exercise authority over a part of the state's territory.[78] Plainly, neither of these definitions applies to the current situation. On September 18, 2001, Congress authorized military action, but it did not issue a declaration of war. Moreover, even if the United States' actions with regard to Afghanistan and the Taliban government amounted to a declaration of war against those entities, the same analysis cannot be applied to groups like Al Qaeda.[79] Al Qaeda is neither a nation nor a government. In fact, those persons being held by the Administration on suspicion of terrorism may be citizens of as many as 47 different nations. A number of these nations are close allies with the United States, such as France, Spain, and Egypt. The decision in *Ex parte Quirn* simply cannot be credibly stretched to cover the present circumstances given current facts and the clear principles of the international law of war.

Furthermore, the Court's decision in *Ex parte Quirn* is now widely recognized as an abysmal model of fairness and justice. Historians who have analyzed FBI records declassified in the 1960s, as well as prosecutors who actually participated in the proceedings, have reached a consensus that the 1942 tribunals were deeply flawed and the fates of those tried were sealed long before the confused proceedings were held.[80] These tribunals certainly should not constitute the model for how the U.S. tries any person for any offense.

Although Congress enacted legislation authorizing the use of courts-martial after the Second World War, such tribunals have limited jurisdiction and have never been used to try offenses committed by civilians.[81] The Supreme Court addressed this issue many years ago in *Ex Parte Milligan*, 71 U.S. 2 (1866), a case in which the Court overturned a conviction of a civilian by a military tribunal because the tribunal had not been authorized either by the Constitution or Congress.[82] Speaking to the issue of Presidential authority, the Court stressed that the use of military tribunals for civilians "cannot [be] justif[ied] on the mandate of the President; because he is controlled by law, and has his appropriate sphere of duty, which is to execute, not to make, the laws; and there is no unwritten criminal code to which resort can be had as a source of jurisdiction."[83] The Supreme Court in the *Milligan* case also expressly rejected the government's contention that the use of a military tribunal was necessary given the exigencies of the Civil War. The Court stressed that "The Constitution of the United States is a law for rulers and people, equally in war and in peace, and covers with the shield of its protection all classes of men, at all times, and under all circumstances."[84]

DOES THE MILITARY ORDER VIOLATE INTERNATIONAL LAW?

To the extent that military commissions can legally hear cases at all, they would be limited to combatants alleged to have violated the laws of war.[85] Violating laws of war, by definition, can only occur during an armed conflict by persons who are acting on behalf of a state or as part of an insurgency that rises to the level of a civil war. Therefore, in order to assess the current situation in terms of international law, we must first determine whether the attacks of September 11, 2001, constituted violations of the laws of war—i.e., were these actions committed during a war by state actors?

Although it appears that under the principles of

BARBARA OLSHANSKY

international law the United States cannot be at war with bands of terrorists, with regard to those fighting on behalf of the Taliban regime, the answer is different. The Taliban regime was the operating government of Afghanistan, whether formally recognized by the United States or not, and once the United States attacked that country, a war was started. Under these circumstances, Taliban fighters captured on the battlefield must be treated in accordance with the requirements of the Geneva Conventions, and therefore, if they are accused of committing war crimes, they must be tried before courts-martial and not military tribunals.

WHAT DOES INTERNATIONAL HUMANITARIAN LAW SAY ABOUT WHO MAY BE BROUGHT BEFORE THE MILITARY TRIBUNALS AUTHORIZED BY THE ORDER? Whether the current situation constitutes a "war" or "armed conflict" within the meaning of international law is of great importance in determining the legal status of those persons involved in the hostilities, the forum in which they can be tried for their actions, and the nature of the charges that can be brought against them. If a state of war exists, then the status of those involved in the September 11 attacks could change from that of civilian to that of combatant. While civilians can be prosecuted for their mere involvement in hostilities, combatants cannot. The status of those captured under international law will either be that of a prisoner of war (POW) protected under the Third Geneva Convention, or that of a civilian or "unprivileged combatant" protected under the Fourth Geneva Convention. The rights afforded to POWs on the one hand, and civilians and unprivileged combatants on the other, differ significantly.[86] For this reason, the question of whether the present state of affairs amounts to an armed conflict must be addressed first.

American officials have used the word "war" to refer to a wide range of governmental programs designed to address major social and political problems—e.g., the "war on poverty" or the "war on drugs"—but historically the word's accepted meaning has been that of a conflict between traditional nations that have defined borders and organized military forces, the success of which is measured in terms of the achievement of geographical objectives. It is from this historical understanding that the definition used in international law is derived.

International humanitarian law imposes rights and obligations on all parties to international and internal armed conflicts. The primary sources of this body of law are the four Geneva Conventions and their two additional protocols.[87] Under international humanitarian law, "war" or "armed conflict" can, by definition, only arise between two or more nation-states or a nation-state and an insurgent group within that state.[88] A "state," for purposes of international law, is "an entity that has a defined territory and a permanent population, under the control of its own government, and that engages in, or has capacity to engage in, formal relations with other such entities."[89] States are the principal entities that have a legal personality in the international legal order; they have the capacity to make agreements and treaties, and they have rights and corresponding obligations under them.

The answer to the question of whether the United States can in fact be "at war" with Al Qaeda or any other group of terrorists is clear in light of these international law principles. Although the United States fits squarely within the definition of a state, terrorist organizations like Al Qaeda plainly do not. Members of the network are reportedly dispersed throughout countries all over the world and are not associated with any distinct territory. Al Qaeda has never been accorded recognition as a state by any other state, and does not have the capacity to engage in relations with other entities.

The absence of a legal state of armed conflict between the United States and Al Qaeda means that those who were involved, either directly or indirectly, in the attacks of September 11 must be considered civilians like Timothy McVeigh and Sheik Abdel Rahman were, and, as such, subject only to this country's criminal jurisdiction, not its military jurisdiction.[90] They cannot legally be brought before and tried by military commissions. The attacks themselves, because they didn't occur in a time of war, cannot by definition be categorized as war crimes. However, because their acts were of such an serious nature, in addition to prosecuting these individuals for their violations of federal and state criminal laws, the government may also prosecute them for engaging in "crimes against humanity," a crime defined by international law.[91]

The international humanitarian law analysis differs for those captured on the battlefield in Afghanistan. Individuals who meet the criteria for combatant status and who are captured in the course of an armed conflict are afforded prisoner of war status, which carries with it a number of rights and protections commensurate with the respect accorded their military status as soldiers. The protections of the Geneva Conventions provide that POWs must be quartered in conditions that meet the same general standards as the quarters available to the captor's force, i.e., the U.S. armed forces. The legal rights of POWs include: (i) the right to attack military objectives (e.g., armed forces personnel, bases, equipment); and (ii) the right not to be prosecuted for legitimate military actions (e.g., taking up arms against other combatants). Those POWs whom the government wishes to prosecute for war crimes (such as the murder of civilians) are entitled to certain minimum standards of due process in judicial proceedings and must be tried by the same court under the same rules as those used for the detaining country's armed forces.[92] In the current conflict, a captured Taliban soldier who fought for the regular armed forces of Afghanistan would likely be deemed a POW, and thus could not be tried by the proposed military commissions.[93] The soldier could, however, be tried by an American court-martial for violations of the laws of war.

Some of the people captured in Afghanistan and detained by the U.S. government may not be POWs. Under the Geneva Conventions, only those who were members of the armed forces or were part of an identifiable militia group that complied with the formal requirements of combatant status may be considered POWs. For example, members of Al Qaeda, who neither wore an insignia or uniform nor complied with the laws of war, may not qualify for POW status. However, in circumstances where there is doubt about a prisoner's status, the Conventions and U.S. military regulations require that the prisoner be considered a POW and treated as such until a "competent tribunal" can make a determination.[94] The presumption that a person captured on a battlefield has POW status provides protections that all nations thought necessary to codify after the Second World War. The U.S. government should embrace this set of rules intended to protect all people, including American servicemen and -women, taken captive in war.

We must also recognize that the rules set forth in the Geneva Conventions require the humane treatment of *all* persons captured during armed conflict. Every captured fighter is entitled to humane treatment including basic shelter, food, clothing, and medical attention.[95] No detainee may be subjected to torture, corporal punishment, or humiliating or degrading treatment. These rules apply regardless of whether one is found to have POW status. If the United States government does not comply with these requirements now and show respect for the Geneva Conventions, it will be in no position to demand that captured American soldiers be treated any better.[96]

WHAT DOES INTERNATIONAL HUMAN RIGHTS LAW SAY ABOUT STRUCTURE AND OPERATION OF THE MILITARY COMMISSIONS AUTHORIZED BY THE ORDER? The Military Order empowers the President to violate the United States' binding international treaty obligations. The International Covenant on Civil and Political Rights (ICCPR), which the United States ratified in 1992, obligates state parties to the Covenant to protect the due process rights of all persons subject to any criminal proceeding. Once these treaty obligations were ratified by the United States they became the "Supreme Law of the Land" under the U.S. Constitution, and must be applied by all courts in proceedings that are brought under them. U.S. treaty obligations cannot simply be overturned by a President who seems to grant himself powers above the law.

The Order is seriously flawed when examined from the perspective of the guarantees and protections afforded by international human rights law. Specifically, the Military Order raises significant concerns regarding whether the United States will comply with its obligations under the ICCPR.[97] Like other agreements ensuring the protection of human rights, the ICCPR permits a country to deviate from some of these obligations in times of public emergencies.[98] However, the Covenant also provides that certain rights and freedoms are *so* fundamental that they may *not* be suspended even in a time of public emergency. These rights include:

➤ the right to live your life (Article 6);
➤ the prohibition against torture and cruel, inhu-

man, and degrading treatment or punishment (Article 7);

➤ the prohibition against slavery (Article 8);
➤ the prohibition against convictions based on retroactive laws (Article 15); and
➤ the right of religious freedom (Article 18).[99]

The Covenant sets forth a specific procedure that must be followed when a State wishes to intentionally infringe upon any of those rights.[100] Under this procedure, a State must immediately inform other parties to the Covenant of the specific provisions from which it has deviated, and must use as intermediary the Secretary General of the United Nations. A State must explain its reasons for the transgression and must state the date upon which it will terminate. Finally, a State may deviate from its obligations under the ICCPR only "to the extent strictly required by the exigencies of the situation" and provided that such measures are not inconsistent with its other obligations under international law.

The terms of the Military Order fall far short of meeting the high standard for violating the human rights guaranteed under the ICCPR. The Order sharply curtails the right to liberty and security of the person as guaranteed by Article 9 of the Covenant, and the right to a fair trial as guaranteed by Article 14 of the Covenant. The Administration has undertaken this derogation even though it has not, and indeed cannot, show that such a suspension of rights is necessary within the current situation, and it has created a military justice system that, as discussed above, will violate other international obligations as well.[101]

THE MILITARY ORDER VIOLATES THE ICCPR'S ARTICLE 9 GUARANTEE OF THE RIGHT TO LIBERTY AND SECURITY OF THE PERSON

Section 2 of the Military Order permits the President to authorize the arrest and detention of people on grounds that are vague and overbroad. The provision allows the military to take a person into custody and try him before a military commission if the President states that he has "reason to believe" that the individual took part in "acts of international terrorism" against the United States. Because the Order fails to define "international terrorism" or to specify the nature of the outlawed conduct, it plainly constitutes an extreme derogation of the Article 9 prohibition against arbitrary arrest and detention. The provision of the Order authorizing military commissions for violations of the laws of war and "other applicable crimes" is flawed for the same reason. In a clear affront to the Convention, this open-ended category would permit the executive branch to try persons for virtually any criminal offense.

The Military Order vests in the Secretary of Defense such unfettered authority to determine the place and length of detention—without any judicial oversight—that it directly undermines Article 9 guarantees. Under Article 9 of the Covenant, an individual detained on a criminal charge must be brought promptly before a judge or officer and is generally entitled to bail pending trial. Under this Article, trial must be held within a reasonable time, and anyone who is detained pending trial has the right to have the lawfulness of the detention determined by a court. But under the President's Military Order, there is no requirement that persons detained be told the reason for their arrest or the charges against them or that they be brought before a judicial authority to determine the lawfulness of their detention. In fact, the Order goes several steps further and expressly negates the right of a detainee to challenge the lawfulness of his detention, makes no provision for bail, and does not mandate that trials be held within a reasonable period of time after the commencement of detention.[102]

THE MILITARY ORDER VIOLATES THE ICCPR'S ARTICLE 14 GUARANTEES OF THE RIGHT TO DUE PROCESS AND TO A FAIR AND PUBLIC HEARING BY A COMPETENT, INDEPENDENT, AND IMPARTIAL TRIBUNAL

Although the Military Order states that trials held by the commissions should be "full and fair," the absence of key due process requirements in the Order indicates that this will not likely be the case. The Order does not provide for a trial by an independent and impartial judge or for a public trial. There is no real privilege against self-incrimination, nor is there any guarantee that defendants will have access to the evidence submitted against them. An individual brought before a military commission will not be entitled to the counsel of his choice.[103] These shortcomings plainly subvert the Covenant's Article 14 guarantees by jeopardizing an accused's right to be informed of the charges against him and to properly prepare a defense.[104]

Equally troubling is the fact that the Military Order does not provide for any appellate review, or even for review by a separate military commission panel. The accused's only recourse is for a review by the President or the Secretary of Defense as the President's designate. All judicial appeals are precluded, including those that might be made to international tribunals.[105] Prominent human rights groups have noted that this denial of the right to appeal under international law is "especially troubling" because the Military Order expressly authorizes that a guilty verdict can lead to a death sentence and secret execution.[106]

Not only does the Order breach Articles 9 and 14, it also undermines several other provisions of the Covenant. In contravention of Article 18's non-derogable guarantee for the right to freedom of religion, Section 3(d) of the Military Order states that detainees will be able to exercise their religion only to the extent "consistent with the requirements of such detention." Similarly, in violation of the nondiscrimination requirements of Articles 2 and 26 of the Covenant, the Order specifies that the military commission system will be applied only to non-U.S. citizens. This discrimination on the basis of national origin violates Article 4 as well.

BARBARA OLSHANSKY

In sum, an analysis of the provisions of the Military Order in light of binding international law reveals that the Order sacrifices the fundamental human rights to personal liberty and a fair trial in ways that far exceed what is permitted under international law even in times of crisis. The Order plainly and unlawfully permits the President to violate our country's binding treaty obligations.

IV

AMERICA'S FOREIGN POLICY WITH REGARD TO THE USE OF MILITARY TRIBUNALS

In virtually every instance in which another country has used military tribunals to try civilians, the United States State Department has strongly criticized the practice and has done so on the specific ground that the elimination of due process guarantees undermines the basic human right to a fair, public trial. Examples of U.S. pronouncements on this issue are abundant.

CHINA

In its annual *Country Report on Human Rights Practices*, the State Department recently criticized the Chinese justice system in part because defendants in China are not provided with certain specific due process guarantees, including the presumption of innocence, proof of guilt beyond a reasonable doubt, and *habeas corpus* relief. In particular, the State Department finds problematic that the Chinese government has broad authority to define crimes that endanger "state security"; that trials involving national security may be conducted in secret, that police can monitor attorney-client meetings; and that defendants are not always permitted to confront their accusers. Most recently, the State Department concluded that "the lack of due process is particularly egregious in death penalty cases."

EGYPT

In its last two Country Reports, the State Department severely criticized the manner in which military tribunals were used in Egypt to try offenses ranging from nonviolent political dissent to acts of terrorism. Specific objections noted by the State Department included the same aspects of military tribunals that are now causing concern in the United States: Civilians may be tried by the military tribunal; the judges are military officers appointed by the Ministry of Defense; and verdicts may not be appealed. The year 2000 annual Country Report issued by the State Department expressly noted that "this use of military courts...has deprived hundreds of civilian defendants of their constitutional right to be tried by a civilian judge." The 2000 report also stated that "military courts do not ensure civilian defendants due process before an independent tribunal" and that the judges "are neither as independent nor as qualified as civilian judges in applying the civilian Penal Code."

The State Department has continually criticized Peru's use of military tribunals to try civilians for treason and terrorism on the grounds that the "proceedings in these military courts—and those for terrorism in civilian courts—do not meet internationally accepted standards of openness, fairness, and due process." Among the specific practices deemed objectionable by the State Department are the holding of treason trials in secret; the prohibition on access to state's evidence files by defense attorneys; and the prohibition on questioning of military and police witnesses. Some of the State Department's strongest language condemning Peru's military trial system was issued during the secret military trial of American citizen Lori Berenson. The State Department protested that the proceeding was not held in "open civilian court with full rights of legal defense, in accordance with international judicial norms."

Just as the United States has repeatedly rejected rationalizations offered by foreign governments for dispensing with due process rights and convening secret military tribunals to try civilians, many political leaders and human rights advocates from inside and outside of the United States have begun to call the Administration to account for putting forth the same unconvincing justifications.[107]

The Administration's rationale for its shocking disregard of official foreign policy pronouncements in this area has been threefold. According to the President, Attorney General Ashcroft, and Vice President Cheney, the military tribunal system is necessary because it will:

(1) ensure swift and uncomplicated justice;
(2) allow the government to "use intelligence information that could not be used in a regular court proceeding"[108] due to concerns about the safety of sources and the confidentiality of intelligence measures; and
(3) ensure the safety of jurors and witnesses.

However, none of these justifications warrants our abandonment of the constitutional court system upon which our ideas of justice are based.

In an attempt to justify its need to depart from the U.S. Constitution at home, the State Department is now repeating some of the same criticisms it has made of military tribunals abroad. The record plainly demonstrates that our federal courts are fully capable of handling cases involving acts of terrorism against the United States.[109] Following public trials that conformed to all constitutional requirements, federal courts convicted the individuals charged with the 1998 bombings of the American embassies in Kenya and Tanzania as well as those charged with the 1993 attack on the World Trade Center. The Administration's argument concerning the necessity of creating military commissions is belied by the fact that Congress has recently expanded the criminal jurisdiction of our federal courts in a deliberate effort to cover a broader range of terrorism offenses.[110] The fact that there have been successful prosecutions of terrorists in our civilian courts lends weight to the growing outcry against the Administration's call for the use of military tribunals.

Moreover, because federal courts are authorized by law to restrict public disclosure of sensitive information and have the power to hold defendants without bond pending trial if their release might cause harm to the national security or endanger the community, neither of these prosecutions jeopardized our intelligence sources or put at risk those serving as jurors or witnesses.[111] Similarly, the Speedy Trial Act ensures that there will not be unreasonable delays in bringing those accused of terrorist acts to justice.

CONCLUSION

The U.S. court system has been acknowledged as one of the world's models for transparent justice in a democratic society. We must not sacrifice our constitutional principles and abandon our commitment to human rights in order to try and punish those found guilty of terrorism.

If the United States government implements the military tribunals authorized by the Military Order, it will undermine our most noble democratic accomplishments in the service of several extremely dubious objectives. First, the government would demonstrate that in the struggle between secrecy and democracy, secrecy will win. The United States would communicate to the world that it is acceptable to replace a fair and open justice system with one that permits one human being to play all of the roles—rule-maker, investigator, accuser, prosecutor, judge, jury, sentencing court, reviewing court, and executioner—and makes no provision for accountability to any other branch of government or to the people. In so doing, the Order will topple the balance of power achieved through centuries of governing, negotiation, and struggle.

Second, by implementing the Military Order, the U.S. would create a model for military (and indeed even civilian) trials devastating in its departure from the principles of due process. We would be creating a system of secret proceedings in which the charges, the evidence, the verdicts, and the punishments would never have to be revealed to the public. Indeed, we will have succeeded in erasing the rulebook of American justice that was painstakingly written during our nation's history and replaced it with a totalitarian code of vengeance.

Third, through the Order's disdain for adherence to fundamental human rights principles in our own country, the U.S. will irrevocably damage our ability to exert leadership and champion human rights around the world. We will have advertised and exported to the world a model that gives license to the most repressive regimes to implement actions that will violate the human and civil rights of their citizens. By implementing these military commissions, the United States will deal a tremendous blow to the institutions of international law. The U.S. will be communicating to the world that it will not comply with the international treaties that it has signed and ratified. We will have etched in bold relief for all to see our dismissal of the collaborative efforts of the world's countries, cultures, and peoples, and our contempt for the results of these efforts.

We must also consider the risks that the military

commission policy poses to Americans living abroad. Once the U.S. uses these tribunals, our government will be unable to protest effectively when other countries seek to use similar measures against American civilians, peacekeepers, diplomats, and soldiers abroad who are accused of terrorist activities.

In taking this treacherous step, the U.S. announces that it rejects our history as a country that was developed by and for immigrants seeking a better life. We will have announced that this country is no longer willing to be a haven—or even a way station—for those who seek refuge from oppression and violence around the globe. Even more startling to those of us who may remember our immigrant grandparents and parents, we will have announced to the world that any person who is not born in this country is inherently suspect.

Yet contrary to what some would have the American citizenry believe, we remain a nation of courageous, open, and tolerant people. We have not forgotten how recently our own families, needing to make new lives because of persecution, drought, famine, or disease, came to this country. And we are neither so ignorant nor so blind as to confuse the word "terrorist" with the word "immigrant."

We will not stray from the path of justice if we are brave and careful and wise in the steps that we take. We must embrace our responsibilities to our communities, and to those struggling for freedom around the world. We cannot accept the devil's bargain that the government is offering, for if we forfeit our commitment to civil and human rights in this campaign born of terror, we disprove the truth of our principles, we undermine our best teachings, and we abandon the ideals that we love best in this country: justice, equality, and truth.

NOTES

1. The November 13 Presidential Order can be found in the Federal Register at 66 Fed. Reg. 57831 (2001). Estimates indicate that the Order applies to more than 20 million non-citizens currently living in the United States, the vast majority of whom are legal residents.

2. *See* Statement of John Bell, special agent in charge of the Detroit FBI office, recounted in "Federal Plans Concern Arab Leaders," Associated Press, November 16, 2001.

3. *See* Interim Rule on *Monitoring of Communications With Attorneys To Deter Acts of Terrorism*, 28 C.F.R. Parts 500 and 501 [BOP-1116; AG Order No. 2529-2001], RIN 11200-ABO8, issued by the United States Department of Justice on October 30, 2001 ("Interim Rule"). The Interim Rule permits the Attorney General, without a prior court order, to authorize the monitoring of all communications between a person in federal custody and that person's lawyer whenever the Attorney General has "reasonable suspicion" to believe that a person "may use communications with attorneys or their agents to further or facilitate acts of terrorism." 28 C.F.R. § 501.3(d). The Interim Rule is applicable to all persons in federal custody, citizens and non-citizens alike. "Terrorism" is not defined in the rule and the notice provision of the rule states that

"all communications between the inmate and attorneys may be monitored, to the extent determined to be reasonably necessary for the purpose of *deterring future acts of violence or terrorism.*" 28 C.F.R. § 501.3(d)(2)(i). (Emphasis supplied.)

4. *See, e.g.*, Memorandum on Government Monitoring of Attorney-Client Communications submitted by lawyers and legal scholars to Attorney General John Ashcroft and Patrick J. Leahy, Chairman of the Senate Committee on the Judiciary, dated December 4, 2001.

5. *See, e.g.*, "Ashcroft Defends Actions to Congress," Reuters, December 6, 2001 (quoting Ashcroft as stating that "[i]f you fit this definition of a terrorist, fear the United States because you will lose your liberties"); Statement of Secretary of Defense Donald H. Rumsfeld and Deputy Secretary of Defense Paul Wolfowitz to the Senate Armed Services Committee (hereafter referred to as the "Rumsfeld Statement"), December 12, 2001, available at: www.defenselink.mil/speeches/2001/s20011212.socdef.html.

6. The Commission Rules can be found on the web at the following address: www.defenselink.mil/news/Mar2002/d20020321ord.pdf.

7. Section 1 of the Commission Rules provides that "supplemental procedures" may be established by the Secretary of Defense pursuant to the Military Order or the Commission Rules. Section 11 of the Commission Rules states that the Secretary of Defense may "amend" the Rules as necessary.

8. *See* Section 2(A) of the Military Order.

9. Unfortunately, the Commission Rules have not clarified this issue in any way.

10. *See* Section 2(A) of the Military Order.

11. Furthermore, as the American Civil Liberties Union has correctly pointed out, the Military Order could easily be extended to include United States citizens who were tried before military commissions during the Second World War. *See* Timothy Edgar, "ACLU Memorandum: President Bush's Order Establishing Military Trials In Terrorism

Cases," November 29, 2001, on file with the author. In the case of *Ex parte Quirin*, 317 U.S. 1 (1942), the Supreme Court held that one of the saboteurs' status as an American citizen did not exempt him from trial before the military commission because he "had violated the law of war by committing offenses constitutionally triable by military tribunal." *Id.* at 44.

12. *See* Rumsfeld Statement to the Senate Armed Services Committee.

13. As discussed further below, civilians living in this country have *always* been found to be entitled to a trial by jury as guaranteed by the Bill of Rights. Our Supreme Court has upheld this principle even in those few cases in which it has approved the use of military commissions. In this way, the Military Order unlawfully extends its reach to persons whom we have never subjected to military justice in this country.

14. Section 2(A)(1) of the Military Order.

15. If, on the other hand, the military commissions create their own criminal code of terrorism offenses and then apply these rules retroactively to try detainees for their violation, the U.S. government would then be violating the constitutional prohibition on *ex post facto* laws. The Constitution expressly prohibits the enactment of a law that provides for the infliction of punishment upon a person for an act done, which, when it was committed, was not unlawful or was not subject to as harsh a punishment as the new law requires. U.S. Constitution, Art. I, § 10.

16. 18 U.S.C. § 2339(B).

17. Section 2(A)(1) of the Military Order. (Emphasis supplied.)

18. *See Gerstein v. Pugh*, 420 U.S. 103 (1975) (holding that the Fourth Amendment requires that arrested persons be afforded a prompt judicial determination of probable cause); *County of Riverside v. McLaughlin*, 500 U.S. 44 (1991) (holding that such determination must be made within 48 hours to comply with the promptness requirement).

19. The Commission Rules issued to implement the Military

Order also fail to define the specific offenses that may be prosecuted by military commission.

20. *See Lanzetta v. New Jersey*, 306 U.S. 451, 59 S.Ct. 618, 83 L.Ed. 888 (1939). The Court recently reaffirmed the vitality of this principle in the criminal context in *Posters `N' Things, Ltd. v. United States*, 511 U.S. 513, 524, 114 S.Ct. 1747 (1997). The due process concerns embodied in the vagueness test are twofold; the doctrine is intended to ensure that (1) citizens are given fair notice of what is prohibited so that they may conform their behavior to the dictates of the law, *Papachristou v. City of Jacksonville*, 405 U.S. 156, 162, 92 S.Ct. 839, 843 (1972), and (2) the discretion of law enforcement officials is limited by explicit legislative standards so as to preclude arbitrary, capricious, and discriminatory enforcement. *See Grayned v. City of Rockford*, 408 U.S. 104, 108–109, 92 S.Ct. 2294, 2299 (1972); *Coates v. City of Cincinnati*, 402 U.S. 611, 614, 91 S.Ct. 1686, 1689 (1971).

21. *See* Section 1(E) of the Military Order.

22. The phrase "common crimes" is a legal term that refers to criminal offenses that are neither war crimes nor political offenses. *See* Joan Fitzpatrick, "The Constitutional and International Invalidity of Military Commissions under the November 13, 2001 'Military Order'" on file with the author.

23. Section 3(B) of the Military Order.

24. Section 4(C)(2) of the Military Order.

25. *See* Sections 4(B) and (C) of the Military Order (authorizing the Secretary of Defense to issue orders and regulations for "the appointment of commissions" and rules "for the conduct of the proceedings of the military commissions, including pretrial, trial, and post-trial procedures, modes of proof, issuance of process, and qualifications of attorneys...").

26. In doing so, the President has clearly violated the Separation of Powers doctrine, and thus usurped one of the most fundamental guarantees of the U.S. Constitution.

27. *See* Rumsfeld Statement to the Senate Armed Services

Committee (stating that "[m]ilitary commissions would permit speedy, secure, fair and flexible proceedings...").

28. *See* Sections 3(A)–(E) and Section 2(B)(2) of the Military Order.

29. USA PATRIOT Act, Section 412; INA Section 236A.

30. *See* Commission Rules, Section 6(D)(3). Our courts have long adhered to the rules of evidence regarding hearsay statements and coerced confessions because of the inherent unreliability of such statements. These exclusionary rules of evidence developed from the notion that the value of a witness's testimony depends on the accuracy of the witness's perception and memory, the witness's ability to present that perception clearly, and the sincerity of the witness. The three conditions under which witnesses are required to testify—oath, personal presence at the trial, and cross-examination—are intended to expose flaws in any of these factors. When a witness recounts the statement of another person who is not present in court, the out-of-court statement of the second person cannot be tested and is not subject to the three conditions designed to ensure accuracy. *See* John W. Strong, *McCormick on Evidence*, Vol. 2, 90–91 (5th ed. 1999).

31. *See Beck v. Ohio*, 379 U.S. 89, 85 S. Ct. 223 (1964) (delineating the probable cause requirement under the Fourth Amendment).

32. *See, e.g., Thompson v. City of Los Angeles*, 885 F.2d 1439 (9th Cir. 1989) (holding that detention for five days before a hearing on probable cause may deprive one of Fourth Amendment rights); *Wayland v. City of Springdale*, 933 F.2d 668 (8th Cir. 1991).

33. *See* Commission Rules, Section 6(D)(1).

34. The Fourth Amendment to the U.S. Constitution states that "the right of the people to be secure in their persons, houses, papers, and effects, against unreasonable searches and seizures, shall not be violated, and no Warrants shall issue, but upon probable cause, supported by Oath or affirmation, and particularly describing the place to be searched, and the persons or things to be seized." This

Amendment has been interpreted by the Supreme Court to safeguard an individual's right to privacy in his home and his person. *See, e.g., Payton v. New York*, 445 U.S. 573, 601 (1980) (holding that "the sanctity of the home...has been embedded in our traditions since the origins of the Republic"); *Skinner v. Oklahoma*, 316 U.S. 535 (1942) (invalidating a state statute that provided for the mandatory sterilization of persons convicted two or more times of "felonies involving moral turpitude").

35. *See* Commission Rules, Section 5(F).
36. The Fifth Amendment to the U.S. Constitution states that "no person shall be held to answer for a capital or otherwise infamous crime unless on presentment by a grand jury, except in cases arising in the land or naval forces, or in the militia, when in actual service in time of war or public danger, nor be deprived of life, liberty, or property, without due process of law." The Fifth Amendment has been interpreted by the Supreme Court to guarantee the right to indictment by a grand jury, prohibit double jeopardy, protect against compulsory self-incrimination, and guarantee due process of law. *See, e.g., Malloy v. Hogan*, 378 U.S. 1 (1964) (upholding the Fifth Amendment right to be free from compelled self-incrimination); *Benton v. Maryland*, 395 U.S. 784 (1969) (upholding the Fifth Amendment right to be free from double jeopardy).
37. The Commission Rules provide that the Presiding Officer of each commission "shall be a military officer who is a judge advocate of any United States armed force," Section 4(A)(4), and that each member of a commission "shall be a commissioned officer of the United States armed forces." Section 4(A)(3). Similarly, the Rules state that both the Chief Prosecutor and the Chief Defense Counsel "shall be a judge advocate of any United States armed force." Section 4(B) and (C).
38. *See* Commission Rules, Section 4(C)(3)(b).
39. *See* Commission Rules, Sections 4(C)(3)(b) and 6(B)(3).
40. *See, e.g., Smalis v. Pennsylvania*, 474 U.S. 140, 106 S. Ct. 1745 (1986) (acquittal); *Harris v. Oklahoma*, 433 U.S. 682,

97 S. Ct. 2912 (1977) (conviction); *Department of Revenue of Montana v. Kurth Ranch*, 511 U.S. 767, 114 S. Ct. 1937 (1994) (multiple punishments).

41. The Sixth Amendment to the U.S. Constitution states that "[i]n all criminal prosecutions, the accused shall enjoy the right to a speedy and public trial, by an impartial jury of the State and district wherein the crime shall have been committed, which district shall have been previously ascertained by law, and to be informed of the nature and cause of the accusation; to be confronted with the witnesses against him; to have compulsory process for obtaining witnesses in his favor, and to have the Assistance of Counsel for his defense."

42. *Duncan v. Louisiana*, 391 U.S. 145, 156, 88 S. Ct. 1444 (1968) (holding the Sixth Amendment right to a jury trial applicable to the states).

43. *See* Commission Rules, Section 6(B)(3).

44. *See* Commission Rules, Section 6(B)(3).

45. *Pointer v. Texas*, 380 U.S. 400, 403, 85 S. Ct. 1065 (1965).

46. *See* Commission Rules, Section 5(A).

47. *See* Commission Rules, Section 5(J).

48. Section 7(A)(1) of the Military Order; Commission Rules, Section 6(D).

49. Section 7(B)(2) of the Military Order.

50. Article I of the U.S. Constitution, which enumerates Congress's powers, includes Section 9, which states:
Clause 2: The Privilege of the Writ of *Habeas Corpus* shall not be suspended, unless when in Cases of Rebellion or Invasion the public safety may require it.

51. *See, e.g., Wong Wing v. United States*, 163 U.S. 228, 238 (1886) (resident aliens entitled to Fifth Amendment rights); *Kwong Hai Chew v. Colding*, 344 U.S. 590, 596 (1953) (resident alien is a "person" within the meaning of the Fifth Amendment); *Mathews v. Diaz*, 426 U.S. 69, 77 (1976) ("There are literally millions of aliens within the jurisdiction of the United States. The Fifth Amendment, as well as the Fourteenth Amendment, protects every one of these persons from deprivation of life, liberty, or property

without due process of law. Even one whose presence in this country is unlawful, involuntary, or transitory is entitled to constitutional protection.") (Citations omitted.)

52. *See Ex parte Quirn*, 317 U.S. 1, 25 (1942); *Yamashita v. United States*, 327 U.S. 1, 9 (1943).

53. *See* Remarks of Chief Justice William H. Rehnquist, 100th Anniversary Celebration of the Norfolk and Portsmouth Bar Association, Norfolk, Virginia, May 3, 2000, *available at* www.supremecourtus.gov/publicinfo/speeches/sp_05-03-00.html.

54. *See Ex parte Merryman*, 17 Fed. Cas. 144, 148 (No. 9487) (C.C.D. Md. 1861) (Chief Justice Taney, sitting as a circuit judge, stated: "I had supposed it to be one of those points in constitutional law upon which there was no difference of opinion,...that the privilege of the writ could not be suspended, except by an act of Congress."). *See also*, Joseph Story, *Commentaries on the Constitution*, 3: §§1333-36 (1883), reprinted in *The Founders' Constitution*, Vol. 1 at 342 (University of Chicago Press, 1987), ("It would seem, as the power is given to congress to suspend the writ of *habeas corpus* in cases of rebellion or invasion, that the right to judge, whether exigency has arisen, must exclusively belong to that body.").

55. The full name of the USA PATRIOT Act is the "Uniting and Strengthening America by Providing Appropriate Tools Required to Intercept and Obstruct Terrorism Act of 2001."

56. USA PATRIOT Act, Section 412.

57. *Ibid.*

58. Although several Administration officials have stated that the Military Order was not intended to prevent individuals detained from seeking writs of *habeas corpus*, no section of the Order reflects these statements. *See, e.g.*, Alberto R. Gonzales, Counsel to the President, "Martial Justice, Full and Fair," *New York Times*, November 30, 2001 (stating that "The order preserves judicial review in civilian courts"). Moreover, other officials have contradicted such statements. *See, e.g.*, *Comments* by Assistant

BARBARA OLSHANSKY

Attorney General Michael Chertoff, ABA Meeting, Washington, D.C., November 29–30, 2001. In any event, in the absence of congressional action or an amendment of the Order, the language of the Order precluding judicial review stands.

59. *See* Section 4(C)(8) of the Military Order.

60. *See* Commission Rules, Section 6(H)(2).

61. U.S. Constitution, Article. II, Section 2.

62. Pub. L. 107–40 (Sept. 18, 2001).

63. 10 U.S.C. §§ 821, 836.

64. U.S. Constitution, Article I, Section 8, Clause 9.

65. U.S. Constitution, Article I, Section 8, Clause 10.

66. U.S. Constitution, Article I, Section 8, Clause 14.

67. Pub. L. 107-40 § 2(a). The Joint Resolution states:
[T]he President is authorized to use all necessary and appropriate force against those nations, organizations, or persons he determines planned, authorized, committed, or aided the terrorist attacks that occurred on September 11, 2001, or harbored such organizations or persons, in order to prevent any future acts of international terrorism against the United States by such nations, organizations or persons.

68. There was no discussion whatsoever of the use of military tribunals during the congressional debate on the Joint Resolution. *See* Cong. Rec. H5638-5683 (Sept. 14, 2001).

69. 10 U.S.C. § 810. Section 810 provides:
The provisions of this chapter conferring jurisdiction upon courts-martial do not deprive military commissions, provost courts, or other military tribunals of concurrent jurisdiction with respect to offenders or offenses that by statute or by the law of war may be tried by military commissions, provost courts, or other military tribunals.

70. 10 U.S.C. § 836. Section 836 provides:
(a) Pretrial, trial, and post-trial procedures, including modes of proof, for cases arising under this chapter triable in courts-martial, military commissions and other military tribunals, and procedures for courts of inquiry, may be prescribed by the President by regulations which shall,

so far as he considers practicable, apply the principles of law and the rules of evidence generally recognized in the trial of criminal cases in the United States district courts, but which may not be contrary to or inconsistent with this chapter.

(b) All rules and regulations made under this article shall be uniform insofar as practicable.

71. *See* 10 U.S.C. Sections 838(b), 852(a), 866, 867, 867(a), and 869.

72. In addition, the Military Order's provision granting exclusive jurisdiction to military commissions conflicts with Congress's specification in Article 18 of the UCMJ that, for purposes of prosecution of the law of war, general courts-martial shall have jurisdiction concurrent with military tribunals. By its terms, the UCMJ applies to prisoners of war Section 802(a)(9), and the Military Order therefore cannot properly claim exclusive jurisdiction over them.

73. *See* Rumsfeld Statement to the Senate Armed Services Committee.

74. These statutes were repealed in 1956 when Congress adopted the current Uniform Code of Military Justice. 10 U.S.C. §§ 1553, 1554 (repealed by Pub. L. 84-1028 (1956)).

75. International humanitarian law or "the laws of war" are designed to protect the life, health, and safety of civilians and other noncombatants (such as soldiers who are wounded or captured) and to delineate boundaries and rules regarding the methods and means by which governments may pursue a war.

76. The U.S. Department of Defense defines the law of war as:

3.1. Law of War. That part of international law that regulates the conduct of armed hostilities. It is often called the law of armed conflict. The law of war encompasses all international law for the conduct of hostilities binding on the United States or its individual citizens, including treaties and international agreements to which the United States is a party, and applicable customary law.

77. The Geneva Convention, Common Article 2 provides that "the present Convention shall apply to all cases of declared war or of any other armed conflict which may arise between two or more of the High Contracting Parties, even if the state of war is not recognized by one of them."

78. Part I, Art. 1(1), Protocol Additional to the Geneva Conventions of 12 August 1949, and Relating to the Protection of Victims of Non-International Armed Conflicts (Protocol II), opened for signature December 12, 1977, 1125 U.N.T.S. 609.

79. Al Qaeda does not have the same control over territory as the Taliban, and it is unlikely that it has a disciplinary system in place through which it could enforce the rules of the law of war.

80. *See, e.g.,* William Carlsen, "A Cautionary Tale From Another War," *San Francisco Chronicle*, November 30, 2001.

81. *See* 10 U.S.C. § 802 (listing people that are subject to the Uniform Code of Military Justice).

82. 71 U.S. 2, 210 (1866). *See* Kathleen Clark, "President Bush's Order on Military Trials of Non-Citizens: Beyond His Constitutional or Statutory Authority," Testimony presented to the U.S. Senate Judiciary Committee Hearing on DOJ Oversight: Preserving Our Freedoms While Defending Against Terrorism, at 2–3 (November 28, 2001).

83. 71 U.S. at 210.

84. 71 U.S. at 209.

85. As discussed below, any use of military commissions may be unlawful under international law even for trying violations of the laws of war.

86. Under international humanitarian law, "combatants" are generally members of the armed forces of a state, but may also include members of militias or volunteer corps forming a part of the armed forces. To be accorded combatant status, one must fulfill certain criteria intended to distinguish the soldier from the general populace, including: (i) be under the command of a responsible superior; (ii) wear a distinctive emblem recognizable at a distance; (iii)

carry arms openly; and (iv) obey the laws and customs of war. The Hague Convention Respecting the Laws and Customs of War on Land, 18 October 1907. Those who do not meet these criteria are referred to as "unprivileged combatants."

87. Geneva Convention for the Amelioration of the Condition of the Wounded Sick in the Field, August 12, 1949 (Geneva I); Geneva Convention for the Amelioration of the Condition of the Wounded, Sick, and Shipwrecked Members of the Armed Forces at Sea, August 12, 1949 (Geneva II); Geneva Convention Relative to the Treatment of Prisoners of War, August 12, 1949 (Geneva III); Geneva Convention Relative to the Protection of Civilian Persons in Time of War, August 12, 1949 (Geneva IV); Protocol Additional to the Geneva Conventions of 12 August 1949 and Relating to the Protection of Victims of International Armed Conflicts, June 8, 1977 (Protocol I); Protocol Additional to the Geneva Conventions of 12 August 1949 and Relating to the Protection of Victims of Non-International Armed Conflict, June 8, 1977 (Protocol II). The United States has ratified all four of the Geneva Conventions but neither of the protocols.

88. Since 1949, international law has recognized that armed conflict can arise within the territory of a single nation. Traditionally, intrastate conflicts, or civil wars, were considered purely matters for the states to handle by themselves, and no international law applied. However, with the adoption of Article 3 common to the four Geneva Conventions, this view was modified.

89. *See* 3rd Restatement on Foreign Relations (1987); Montevideo Convention of 1933.

90. In the absence of a state of war or armed conflict, the categories of combatant and unprivileged combatant are not applicable.

91. The most recent authoritative definition is provided in the Statute of the International Criminal Court. Article 7, Section 1 of the Statute states that "crimes against humanity" means "any of the following acts when committed as

part of a widespread or systematic attack directed against any civilian population, with knowledge of the attack: (a) Murder; (b) Extermination; (c) Enslavement; (d) Deportation or forcible transfer of population; (e) Imprisonment or other severe deprivation of physical liberty in violation of fundamental rules of international law; (f) Torture; (g) Rape, sexual slavery, enforced prostitution, forced pregnancy, enforced sterilization, or any other form of sexual violence of comparable gravity; (h) Persecution against any identifiable group or collectivity on political, racial, national, ethnic, cultural, religious, gender...,or other grounds that are universally recognized as impermissible under international law, in connection with any act referred to in this paragraph or any crime within the jurisdiction of this Court; (i) Enforced disappearance of persons; (j) The crime of apartheid; (k) Other inhumane acts of a similar character intentionally causing great suffering, or serious injury to body or to mental or physical health."

92. *See* Geneva Conventions; Uniform Code of Military Justice.

93. Secretary of Defense Rumsfeld has suggested that this rule should not apply to persons fighting for the Taliban government because the Taliban was not internationally recognized as the government of Afghanistan. The Secretary's suggestion has no legal or political support. Neither the Geneva Conventions nor the United States has ever made or recognized such a distinction. For example, during the Korean War, neither the United States nor the United Nations recognized the government of communist China; nevertheless U.S. forces treated Chinese prisoners as POWs.

94. Indeed, the Pentagon's *Judge Advocate General Handbook* contains the same admonition: "when doubt exists" about a prisoner's status, "tribunals must be convened" to make a determination.

95. Amnesty International has reported that thousands of prisoners in Afghanistan are at risk from hunger, dysentery, pneumonia, and hepatitis, and that the overcrowded prison

camps are suffering from severe shortages of food, medical supplies, and adequate shelter against the harsh conditions of winter. The conditions there, as well as those in Camp X-Ray paint a terrible picture of America's descent to inhumane law enforcement measures.

96. During the Vietnam War, the United States sought revisions in the Geneva Protocols specifically to ensure that any persons captured in war are protected by the treaties whether they were civilians, military personnel, militia, or fell into none of these categories.

97. In ratifying this Covenant, the United States undertook an obligation to respect and uphold the international human rights guaranteed by the Covenant, not only for its own citizens, but for "all individuals within its territory and subject to its jurisdiction...without distinction of any kind, such as race, colour, sex, language, religion, political or other opinion, national or social origin, property, birth or other status." ICCPR, Article 2.

98. Article 4 of the ICCPR provides that a country may derogate from the Covenant's obligations when: (i) there is a "time of public emergency which threatens the life of the nation," (ii) the existence of such a state of affairs is "officially proclaimed," (iii) the derogation is limited to "the extent strictly required by the exigencies of the situation," (iv) the measures taken are not "inconsistent with their other obligations under international law," and (v) the measures taken do not "involve discrimination solely on the ground of race, colour, sex, language, religion or social origin."

99. If the President or the Secretary of Defense were to adopt a code of offenses to be tried by military commission and then apply these laws retroactively, the United States would then be in the position of having violated the nonderogable right to be free from *ex post facto* laws.

100. ICCPR, Article 4(3).

101. ICCPR, Article 4(1) and (2).

102. Section 7(2) of the Military Order.

103. Indeed, the Order also leaves unspecified the extent to

which a defendant will be able to communicate with defense counsel.

104. ICCPR, Article 14(3)(a) and (b).

105. The Military Order provides that one charged under it "shall not be privileged to seek any remedy or maintain any proceeding, directly or indirectly, or to have any such remedy or proceeding sought on the individual's behalf" before a U.S. court, "a court of any foreign nation," or "any international tribunal." Section 7(B).

106. *See, e.g.,* November 15, 2001 Letter of Kenneth Roth, Executive Director of Human Rights Watch, to President George W. Bush, available at www.hrw.org.

107. *See, e.g.,* "UN Rights Head Backs Afghan Probe, Criticizes U.S.," Reuters, December 7, 2001 (reporting the concerns of U.N. Human Rights Chief Mary Robinson about the lack of safeguards built into the military order); "U.S. Heads for Civil Liberties Showdown," Reuters, November 30, 2001 (reporting that several foreign governments, including Spain, "have come out strongly against the use of military tribunals").

108. Statement of Vice President Cheney as reported in "Bush Defends Investigation Tactics," Associated Press, November 30, 2001.

109. *See, e.g.,* Peter A. Schey, "Marching the War on Terrorism Towards Injustice: Military Tribunals and Constitutional Tunnels," Publication of the Center for Human Rights and Constitutional Law, November 30, 2001.

110. *See, e.g.,* Omnibus Diplomatic Security and Antiterrorism Act of 1986, 18 U.S.C. § 2331 (providing federal courts with extraterritorial jurisdiction over terrorist acts committed abroad against U.S. nationals); Antiterrorism and Effective Death Penalty Act of 1996, 18 U.S.C. § 2332b (creating a new federal offense penalizing acts of terrorism that transcend national boundaries).

111. *See, e.g.,* 18 U.S.C. § 3521. The government has also employed special procedures to safeguard the identity of jurors, and the Bail Reform Act authorizes courts to detain a defendant pending trial.

BARBARA OLSHANSKY is the Assistant Legal Director of the Center for Constitutional Rights. Barbara's current docket at the Center includes class action lawsuits concerning immigrants' rights, race discrimination in employment and education, environmental justice and public health, prisoners' rights, and Native American rights.

THE CENTER FOR CONSTITUTIONAL RIGHTS is a nonprofit legal and educational organization dedicated to protecting and advancing the rights guaranteed by the United States Constitution and the Universal Declaration of Human Rights. CCR's work began in 1966 with the legal representation of civil rights activists in the Jim Crow South. Over the last four decades, CCR has played an important role in many popular movements for peace and social justice. CCR uses litigation proactively to combat government efforts to suppress political dissent, to advance the law in a positive direction, to empower poor communities and communities of color, to train the next generation of constitutional and human rights attorneys, and to strengthen the broader movement for constitutional and human rights.

Center for Constitutional Rights
666 Broadway, 7th Floor
New York, NY 10012
(212) 614-6464 | www.ccr-ny.org

**AVAILABLE SOON FROM THE
OPEN MEDIA PAMPHLET SERIES**

SILENCING POLITICAL DISSENT

How Post-September 11 Anti-Terrorism
Measures Threaten Our Civil Liberties

BY NANCY CHANG

FOREWORD BY HOWARD ZINN

"In a crude exploitation of the anguish and concern over the terrorist atrocities of September 11,
the Bush administration has sought to implement
favored programs that have no relation to terrorism and would be sure to arouse protest if it could
not cynically wield the weapon of 'patriotism' to
silence opposition. That includes steps to
strengthen unaccountable executive power and
curb independent thought and expression. Chang's
study expertly reviews these threats, which should
be understood and resisted by those who value
their freedom and democratic rights."

—Noam Chomsky

ISBN: 1-58322-494-7 | $6.95 | www.sevenstories.com